the true book

LIBRARY OF SCIENCE

and Fascinating Facts

Prepared under the direction of
Illa Podendorf, Laboratory School
University of Chicago.

CHILDRENS PRESS, CHICAGO

CONTENTS

The TRUE BOOK Library

A set of books for the primary grades covering 30 factual subjects to spark development of young minds by encouraging early independent reading. All are written in an interesting, easy-to-understand manner, carefully graded for earliest reading levels. Subjects appealing to every interest with story continuity containing well-organized, constructive information that will provide the young reader with excellent tools to grasp facts on a great variety of down-to-earth subjects.

Curious young minds will enjoy these delightful stories written in large, clear, manuscript type with numerous illustrations. Carefully controlled vocabularies for broadest use — 98% of words used are from Combined List for Primary Reading.

Childrens Press, Inc.
1961 Printing
Printed in the U. S. A.

Prepared under the direction of
Illa Podendorf

Laboratory School, University of Chicago

Ninety-eight per cent of the text is in words from
the Combined Word List for Primary Reading

the true book of

MOON
SUN
and
STARS

By John Lewellen

Pictures by Lois Fisher

PREPARED UNDER THE DIRECTION OF ILLA PODENDORF,
LABORATORY SCHOOL, UNIVERSITY OF CHICAGO.
NINETY-EIGHT PER CENT OF THE WORDS USED ARE FROM
THE COMBINED WORD LIST FOR PRIMARY READING.

Childrens Press, Chicago

TABLE OF

CONTENTS

When you look at the sky
at night, something plays
a trick on you.
The moon looks bigger
than the stars.

The moon is much smaller
than the stars and the
sun.
It is much smaller than the
earth.

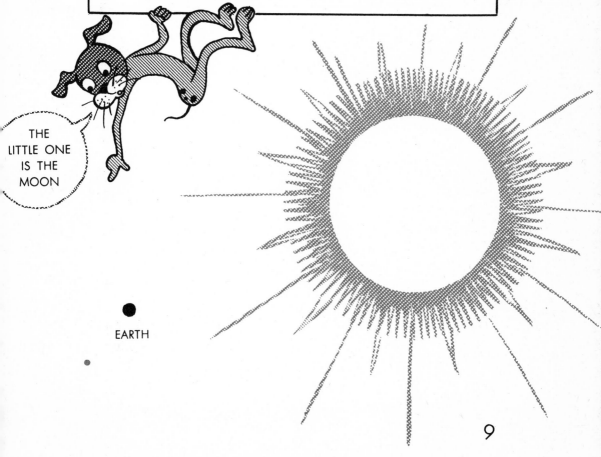

THE
LITTLE ONE
IS THE
MOON

EARTH

But the moon is much
closer to us than any
star.
It is closer than the sun.
That is why it looks so big.
Hold a penny close to
your eye.
It looks big.
Look at it across the room.
It looks small.

The moon moves around
the earth. It makes one
trip in about four weeks.
We never see the other
side of the moon.
No one ever has. A space
ship may take us to the
other side some time.

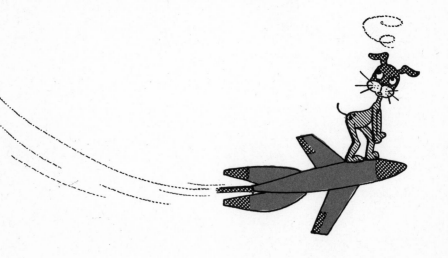

MOON MOVES AROUND EARTH LIKE THIS

EARTH MOVES AROUND SUN LIKE THIS

13

The moon looks flat to us.
But it is a round ball, like
the earth.
The moon is not made of
green cheese.
It is made of rock.
People once thought there
was a "man in the moon"
What looks like "a man in
the moon" are
mountains
and holes
and flat rocks.

14

Also, the moon would be
too hot or too cold.
Days and nights on the
moon are two weeks
long.
Our days are not so hot
as days on the moon.
If they were, our rivers
and lakes would boil.
Our nights are not so cold
as nights on the moon.
If they were, none of our
plants and animals
could live.

People once
thought the
moon had fires
on it.
They thought the
fires made it
bright.
Now we know the
moon is like a
mirror.
It gets its light from
the sun.

We see only that
part of the moon
lighted by the
sun.
The rest of the
moon is there,
but most of the
time it is too
dark to be seen.
That is why the
moon seems to
change its shape
during the month.

You can see how this
works with a ball.
Let the ball be the moon.
Let your head be the earth.
Let the light be the sun.
Turn around with the ball.

You will see the shapes of
the moon.
The ball also shows why
we see only one side of
the moon.
As you turned with the
ball, you saw the same
side of the ball all the
way around.
The moon turns around
once itself while going
around the earth. The
ball did the same thing.
We see only one side.

The earth shines,
too. The earth is
like a mirror, too.

If you were on the moon,
the earth would look
bright when the sun was
shining on it.
It would look much like
the moon, but bigger.

The light of the moon
   comes from the sun.
Our daylight comes from
   the sun.
What is the sun?
The sun is a star. The stars
   we can see have their
   own light.
There are many big stars
   we can not see. Their
   light has burned out.
   Others are still bright,
   but they are so far

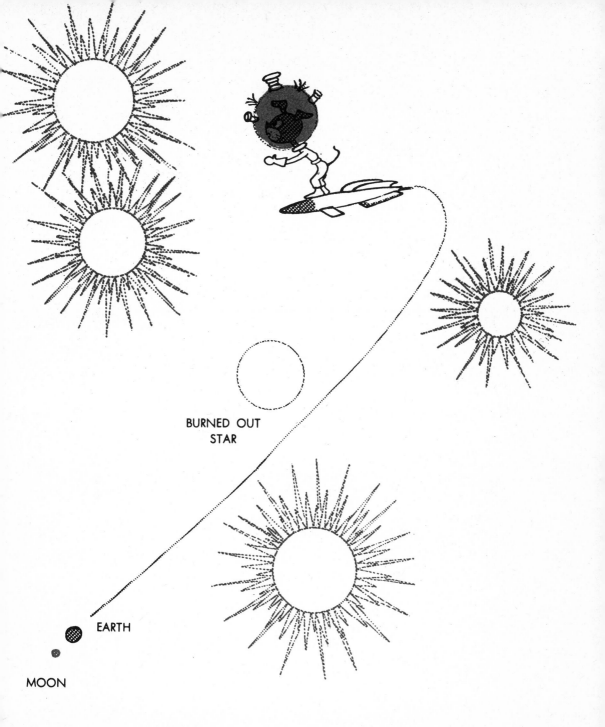

BURNED OUT
STAR

EARTH

MOON

25

away we can not see
them.

The sun looks bigger than
other stars because it is
closer to us.

The sun and other stars
we see are very hot.

They are like great balls
of fire.

The sun is far away. And
the air around us saves
us from the heat of the
sun. The air keeps the
earth from getting as
hot as the moon.
The moon has no air.

27

Many stars are in the sky
  all day.
They are far away.
The sun is closer and its
  light is much brighter.

It is so bright we can not
  see the other stars in
  the daytime.
Part of the time the moon
  is in the daytime sky, too.
Sometimes it is bright
  enough to see during
  the day.

The sun is a star, but we do not see it at night.

At night it is on the other side of the earth. If you took a fast airplane at night to the other side of the earth, you would see the sun. It would be day there. It would be night here.

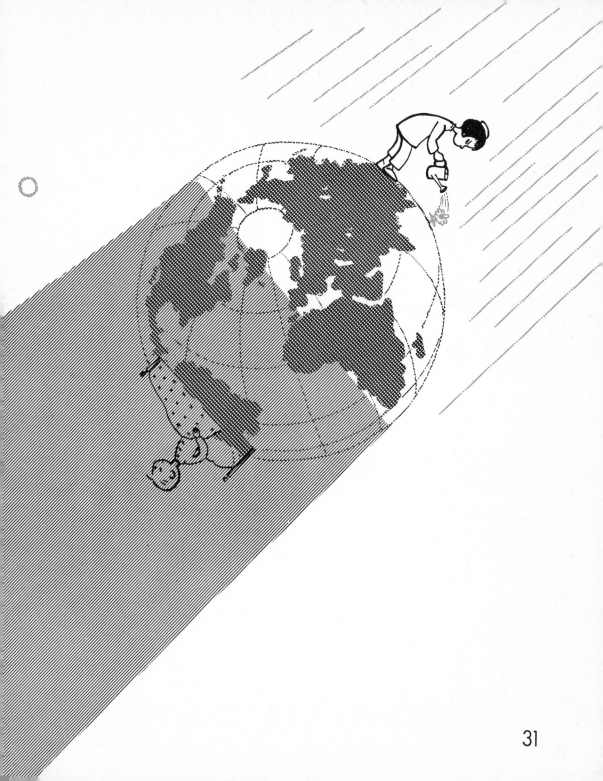

Did you see the sun set
    last night? The sun does
    not move when it sets.
We are the ones that
    move.
As we turn, it looks as if
    the sun were setting.
When the earth turns far
    enough, we can not see
    the sun.
Then we say it is night.

33

The moon turns around
once in about four
weeks.
The earth turns all the
way around once in
one day and one night.
You turn with the earth,
but you do not fall off.

If you were here when you
had your breakfast...

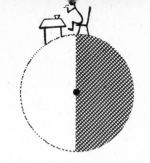

VIEW
FROM
SPACE
ABOVE
NORTH
POLE

you would be here when
you have your lunch...

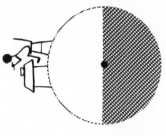

here at bedtime...

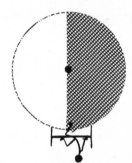

here in the middle of
the night...

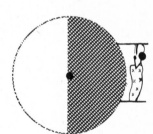

and back here for breakfast
the next morning.

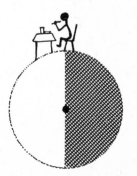

The earth holds you to it.
You do not feel upside
down.
"Down" points to the
middle of the earth.
Your feet point "down."

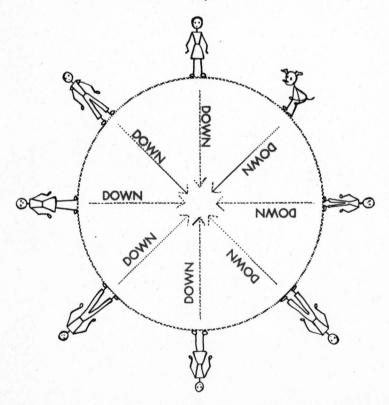

You do not feel yourself
move as the earth turns.
That is because the air
and everything around
you turns with you.
You move very, very fast.
The earth turns as fast as
most jet airplanes fly.

The earth goes even faster
in another way. It moves
around the sun. We
take the moon with us.
It takes our earth one year
to go around the sun.
Because it goes around
the sun, the earth is
called a "planet."
There are eight other
planets that go around
the sun, too. We are
like one big family in
the sky.

MERCURY

 VENUS

EARTH

MARS

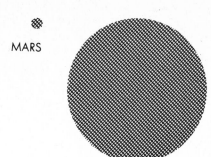

JUPITER

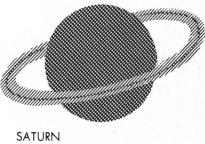

SATURN

URANUS

NEPTUNE

PLUTO

We know more about the
earth than any other
planet.
The other planets shine
with the sun's light, just
as the earth and the
moon do.
Planets look like stars in
the sky. But stars twinkle.
Planets do not.
Two planets, Venus and
Mars, sometimes can be
seen in the daytime.

41

Planets and stars are
round like giant balls.
They do not have points
on them. The air makes
them look that way.

42

A "shooting star"
is not a real star.
It is a bit of rock
or stardust falling
through space. It
burns bright with
the heat it makes

as it passes through
the air around the
earth.

The sun gives us light and warmth. It makes plants grow and makes leaves green. It draws up water into clouds so it can rain.

The moon lights the earth at night.

Planets and stars help ships and airplanes find their way at night.

All are wonderful to see!

*Factual information for curious young minds,
designed for independent reading with 98% of
the text in words from the Combined Word List
for Primary Reading*

the true book of

A I R

AROUND US

by Margaret Friskey
pictures by Katherine Evans

CHILDRENS PRESS
Chicago

CONTENTS

"This Edition Printed - - 1961
Copyright, 1953, Childrens Press
Printed in the U.S.A.

AIR AROUND US

The band of air
   around the earth
   is about 200 miles high.
The heaviest part of it
   is close to the earth.
Here, close to the earth,
   winds are born.
Here there is sound and weather.
Here we can live.
Here we can be warm.
Eight miles up the air is always cold.
Fifty miles up the air is too thin
   to carry sound. It is too thin
   to breathe.

If the earth were a ball this big,
the band of air around it
would be only this wide.

Outside the band of air, it is dark.
The bright eye of the sun,
   like a great spotlight,
   reaches through the dark.

There are all colors in light.
Sunlight, going through a prism,
    breaks into all of its colors.
When sunlight hits the air
    around the earth,
    the light bends a little.
We see the blue.
We see blue in the sky because of
    the air.
The air spreads the sunlight
    across the earth.
The air saves us from some
    of the burning light.

10

The heavy air, near the earth,
   has dust and smoke and water vapor in it.
The light of a sunset comes across
   through this heavy air.
The light is bent a little more.
We see the reds and gold in the light.
There is wonder in the air around us.

WIND

Wind is moving air.
The wind can be a friendly thing.
It can dry the clothes. It picks up
the water and carries it away. This
is called *evaporation*.

It can move a boat

and lift a kite

and help an airplane

and carry seeds

and bring the rain.

Why does the wind blow?
Warm air spreads out.
Now it is lighter.
It goes up.
Heavy cool air moves in
    to take its place.
The air is always moving.

The sun shines THROUGH the air.
The sun warms the earth
    and things on it.
The earth warms the air.
This is one reason high air is so cold.
Some mountains have snow
    on them
    all summer.

Some parts of the earth are always cold.
Some parts are always hot.

The sun is closer to some parts of the earth.
It shines straight on them. There it is hot.

16

The sun warms the earth and things on it.
Even in the same place
  things warm up in different ways.
Put a cookie pan and a wooden bread board
  side by side in the sun.

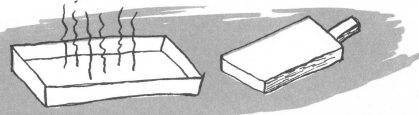

The pan warms up more quickly.
But the board will stay warm longer
  after the sun sets.

A field of wheat gives up more warmth
  to the air than a cool dark woods.

Sand in the sun grows hot.

The water is cool.

The warm air above the sand goes up.

The cool air over the sea moves in.

Dig down in the sand a little. It is cold.

The warmth is all on top.

At night, the land cools quickly.

But the water has taken the sun's warmth
  deep into it.

The wind changes. Cool air blows off the land.

So the earth, warming and cooling the air,
  keeps it moving around.

The air is never still.

HURRICANES

A hurricane is a big wind storm.
It is always born over water.
The sun beats down for days and days
 on a quiet sea in a warm part of the world.
A lot of hot air goes up.

When this hot air meets cold air,
   they begin to roll around faster and faster.
The winds can build up to 100 miles an hour.
The storm can be 200 miles wide.
It begins to move. Word of it is sent out.
People in its path board up their windows.
They tie up their boats.
Even the little animals feel the storm
   coming in the air.
They scoot off to the cover of the deep woods.

Cyclones and tornadoes are wind storms, too.
They build up over the hot land.
But they are much smaller than a hurricane.
All such wild wind storms come from the
meeting of very hot and very cold air.

WEATHER MAPS

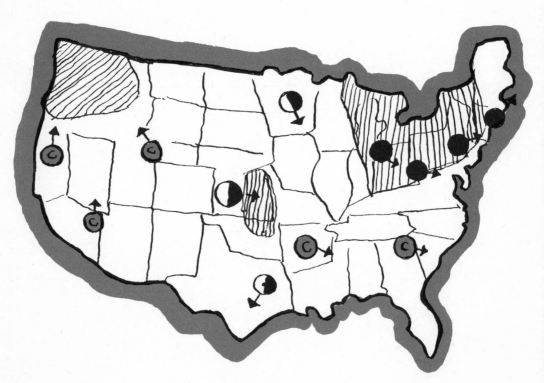

Air is always moving because warm air is
going up and cool air is moving in.
The weatherman can show where wind is
building up. He can show the way
he thinks it will move.

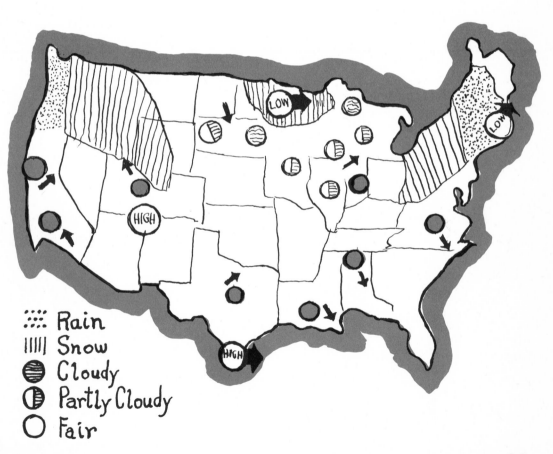

:::: Rain
||||| Snow
⊜ Cloudy
◐ Partly Cloudy
○ Fair

CLOUDS

A cumulus cloud is the soft head
   on a neck of warm air
   that is moving up.
There is water vapor in the air.
It cools as it goes up and changes
   to droplets.
Cumulus clouds are beautiful
   fair weather clouds.

Air moving up and moving down
   under a cloud
   makes bumpy flying for an airplane.

Cirrus clouds are high clouds.

They are 8 to 10 miles high.

They are thin strings of ice and snow.

They move very fast.

Often they are running before a storm.

26

A "mackerel sky" has both
   cirrus and cumulus clouds.
Such a sky means rain is coming.

27

Stratus clouds are low and dark.

Cumulus clouds have grown thick and heavy.

They cover the whole sky.
It looks like rain.

LIGHTNING

Everything in the world has some
electricity in it.
Most of the time it stays quiet.
Rub your feet over a wool rug. Touch
a metal door knob. There is a little
spark. You picked up some parts of
the electricity in the rug. It jumps
to the door knob and gets back to the
rug.

A thunderhead is a big, dark cloud
  with wild winds in it.
Rain and hail and snow and sleet are there.
They are thrown up and down in the cloud
  as though they were shaken up in a big bag.
They are broken apart.
Electricity is built up.
There is too much of it to be quiet.
It wants to jump.
It is not easy for electricity to move
  through air.
But the electricity in the cloud seems
  to feel around until it finds a path
  of air that it can move through.
Then it jumps to another cloud,
  or to the earth.

Lightning is electricity jumping
through the air.
For the air, it is good and wonderful.
The air has a gas in it that is called
ni-tro-gen.
Plants must have nitrogen to grow.
They can't always get it from the air.
Lightning changes this nitrogen so that
rain can carry it to the ground. Plants
can get it through their roots.
Loads and loads of nitrogen make the land
rich because of lightning in the air.

Thunder is only the noise that air makes
  when lightning jumps through it.
Lightning is very, very hot.
The air it moves through gets hot, too.
This hot air spreads out and takes up
  more space. Then it cools again and
  comes back to size. More air rolls in.
This noise the air makes is thunder.
Some of the rolling noise is only sound
  jumping back and forth from hills and clouds

RAIN

There is always water in the air.
It cannot be seen.
But look at a cold glass of lemonade on
a hot day.
The water vapor in the air around the cold
glass cools. It changes into droplets.
These come together on the cold glass. The
outside of the glass is wet.
In a cloud, droplets have come together
around bits of dust.
When the cloud cools more, the droplets
come together to make raindrops.
When a cloud is cool enough and heavy enough,
the rain falls.
The Hopi Indians did a dance with rattle-
snakes to try to make it rain.

Rainmakers, now, try to make it rain, too.

They send up smoke that takes a kind of dust
  to the cloud for raindrops to be made on.

Sometimes a flier goes over a cloud and
  drops bits of dry ice into it
  to cool it.

These rainmakers know that when a cloud is
  heavy enough with raindrops and cool
  enough, it will rain.

If a cloud is just about ready to rain,
  it can sometimes be knocked into it.

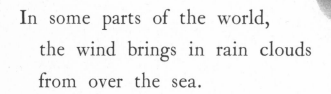

In some parts of the world,
   the wind brings in rain clouds
   from over the sea.

Then the wind takes the clouds up as it
   goes over the mountains.
As the clouds go up, they cool.
They drop their rain.

36

There is no rain for the far side
of the mountains.
Here it is dry and sandy.

In all the air and all the earth,
  there is just so much water.
There is never any more.
None is ever lost, or gained.
The earth and the air keep giving it
  to each other.
A cloud picks up rain as it moves over
  a lake, by evaporation of water in
  the lake.
It drops it on a cornfield, miles away.
The cornfield gives back many pails of
  water to the air every day.

Oceans, rivers, lakes,
    a line full of clothes,
    all give water to the air.
There could be no rain without the air
    to store it up and carry it and drop it.

FOG

Fog is an earth cloud.
Air, heavy with water vapor, cools.
The vapor changes to droplets.
These get on bits of dust.
A little hot sun will clear the air.

HAIL

Hail sometimes follows
a summer thunder storm.
High air is cold.
Hot air carries the raindrops up
into the cold air. They turn to ice.
They start to fall, but meet warm air
coming up.
The ice balls take on more raindrops
and are thrown up into the cold air again.
Hail is bumped up and down in the warm and
cold air. When it is too heavy to be
carried up, it falls to earth.
Hail stones can be so big they hurt
the fields and fruit trees.

SLEET

Sleet begins to fall as rain.
It turns to ice in cold air near the earth.

SNOW

Snow is made in the high clouds.
Droplets, too small to be seen,
  turn into bits of ice.
Many of these bits of ice come together
  to make a snowflake.
A snowflake always has six points.
It is a beautiful thing of air and ice
  that softly comes to earth.

OTHER FACTS ABOUT AIR

You cannot see the air, or taste it
or smell it. But you always have to
have it. It is real. It takes up space.

Air has gases in it.

It has oxygen, nitrogen, carbon dioxide
and water vapor in it.

You draw air into your lungs about
20 times every minute.

People and animals use the oxygen in the
air. They breathe out the carbon dioxide.

Plants breathe air through little holes
in the leaves. The leaves use the carbon
dioxide. They give off the oxygen.

At sea level, air is pressing on us from
all sides at the rate of 15 pounds a
square inch.

Twenty miles up, the air is thin. The
pressure is only 2½ ounces per square inch.

Air protects us from bits of rock and star
dust falling through space.
These bits—shooting stars—hit the earth's
air and burn to dust from friction.

We could have no life on earth without
the friendly, moving, unseen band of air
around us.

The "True Book" series is prepared
under the direction of
Illa Podendorf
Laboratory School, University of Chicago
Ninety-eight per cent of the text is in words from
the combined Word List for Primary Reading

the true book of

SEASONS

by **ILLA PODENDORF**

pictures by **MARY GEHR**

CHILDRENS PRESS

Chicago, Illinois

TABLE OF

"This Edition Printed ----1961"
Copyright, 1955, Childrens Press
Printed in U.S.A.

CONTENTS

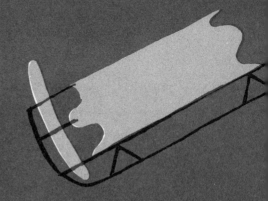

THE SUN AND THE SEASONS

There are four seasons
in a year. They are:

Spring

Summer

Fall

Winter

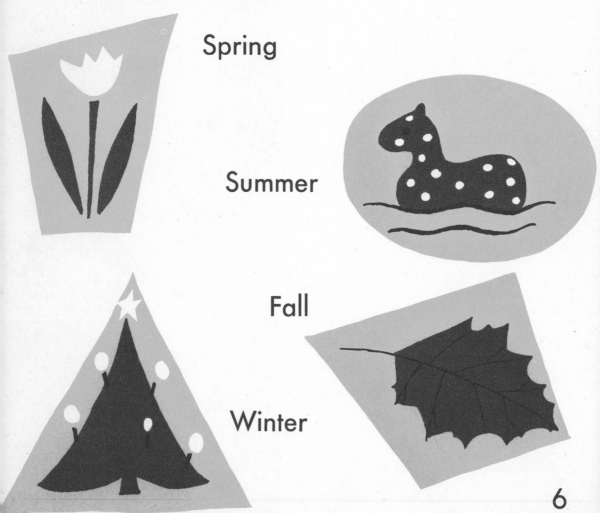

We have seasons because
the earth goes around the sun
and because the earth
is tipped.

It takes the earth a year
to go once around the sun.

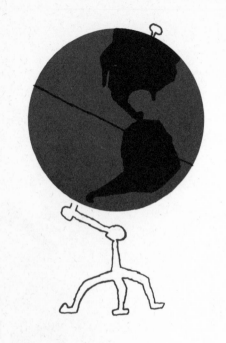

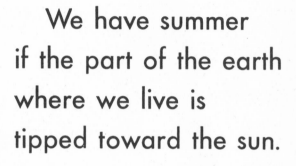

We have summer
if the part of the earth
where we live is
tipped toward the sun.

We have winter
if the part of the earth
where we live is
tipped away from the
sun. The sunshine
is on more of a
slant.

When we have summer our shadows are short at noontime.

When we have winter our shadows are long at noontime.

9

In some parts
of the world it is
warm almost
all year.

In some parts
of the world it is
cold almost
all year.

SPRING

Janet and Jim live in a part of the world where the weather changes with the seasons.

They are glad to see spring come.
Snow melts.
Grass turns green.
The days grow warmer.

It gets light earlier
in the morning.

It stays light later
in the evening.

Robins and many other
kinds of birds return from
the south where they have
been all winter.

Birds build nests and
eggs are hatched.

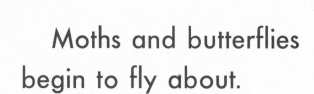

Moths and butterflies
begin to fly about.

Toads come up out of
the ground after their
long winter sleep and
hunt for food.

Buds on the trees swell
and break into leaves
and flowers.

Farmers plow their fields
and get them ready to plant
their crops.

People work in their gardens.
As soon as the ground is ready,
they plant the seeds.

There are spring showers
and warm sunshine.
Flowers burst into bloom.

17

Children bring out
their roller skates,
jumping ropes,
and baseballs and bats.

SUMMER

Janet and Jim like summer
almost as much as spring.
The weather is warm.
Sometimes it is hot and it
is fun to go to the beach.

19

The days are longer than at
any other time of the year.
There is more time for picnics.

Sometimes Janet and Jim
go camping in the summer
time.

Mother and father birds are busy hunting food for their babies.

22

Almost everywhere
animals are busy caring
for their babies.

23

Warm rain and bright sunshine
make the gardens grow.

Soon there are many ripe
vegetables in them.

Farmers harvest their
wheat crops in the summer.

They cut their hay.

25

Fall comes. The days grow
shorter. Leaves turn color.
Some turn yellow. Some
turn red.

Janet and Jim help to rake
the fallen leaves.

Many kinds of plants
scatter their seeds in the fall.

Many animals get ready for
winter.

Squirrels gather nuts and
hide them.

Toads eat a great deal to be
ready to go down into the
ground when winter comes.

Bears and raccoons
grow fat so they can
sleep most of the
winter.

Geese fly over,
going south.
Many kinds of birds
go south
in the fall.

30

Beavers store food and
make their homes ready
for cold weather before
the ponds freeze over.

Farmers gather in the
corn from their fields.

Many trees in
orchards are full
of ripe fruit in
the fall.

The fruit must
be carefully picked
and packed.

People store fruits and
vegetables for winter.

Mothers can some of them
so they will not spoil.

Some fruits and vegetables
are put in a freezer.

They will not spoil if
they are properly frozen.

Farmers store food for their animals to eat in the winter time.

The cool fall air is hazy with smoke from burning leaves.

Boys play football.

WINTER

It is real cold in
winter time.

Janet and Jim must wear
warm clothing.

Horses and some other animals
grow warm coats of fur and
can be out in winter weather.

There is much snow in the
winter time. Janet and Jim
like to play in it.

They build a snowman and
they build a fort.

Sometimes wind piles snow
in high drifts. Janet and
Jim help shovel the walks.

Snow plows push the
snow off streets and
highways.

Bears and some other animals
sleep in their dens most of
the winter.
They almost never go out for
food because they ate a
great deal in the fall.

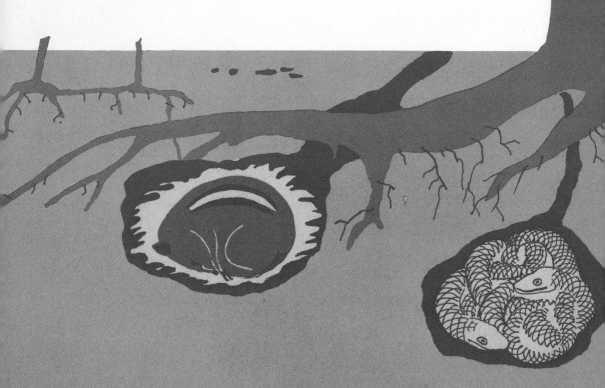

Bulbs and roots of plants rest in the ground under the snow.

The snow helps to keep them from freezing. Seeds rest in the ground under the snow, too.

Snow has lots of air in it. It is the air which helps to keep the bulbs, roots, and seeds from freezing.

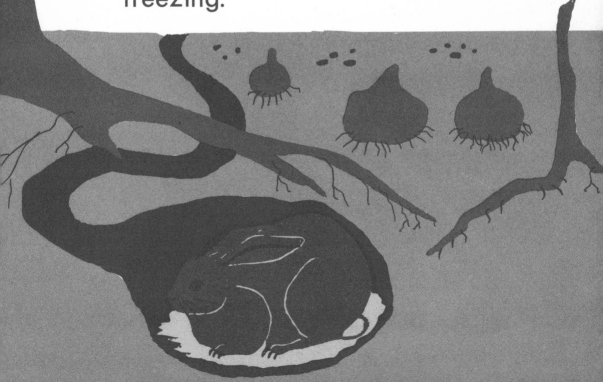

The children coast on the
snowy hills.
They skate on the frozen ponds.

The very shortest day of the year is in the winter time.

It is dark when the children have their supper. It is dark when they get up in the morning.

At last the days become a little longer.

The snow begins to melt and the moisture goes down into the ground.

The sunshine is on less and less of a slant. It is warmer and warmer.

When Janet and Jim
see their first robin,
they think spring
has come again.

47